QUICK LANGUAGES

MULTI-LANGUAGE PHRASEBOOK COLLECTION

AMERICAN BOOK GROUP

ENGLISH-TURKISH
TURKISH-ENGLISH

GET THE AUDIOVISUAL AND INTERACTIVE CONTENT AT **QuickLanguages.com**

QUICK LANGUAGES

MULTI-LANGUAGE PHRASEBOOK COLLECTION

SPEAK ANY LANGUAGE NOW!

WHAT IS QUICK LANGUAGES?

Did you know that we only use about 1,000 words in our everyday vocabulary? The same goes for any language! So, mastering a digital phrasebook with interactive pronunciation tools is a smart alternative to long and expensive language instruction.

Quick Languages is an interactive phrasebook that introduces you to the 12 predominant world languages all in one convenient drop-down menu. Designed for visual, auditory, and kinesthetic learners alike, it is simple, affordable, and effective.

Own the potential of connecting with over 3 billion people!

GET THE AUDIOVISUAL AND INTERACTIVE CONTENT AT
QuickLanguages.com

QUICK LANGUAGES

MULTI-LANGUAGE PHRASEBOOK COLLECTION

SPEAK ANY LANGUAGE NOW!

QUICK LANGUAGES PHRASEBOOK COLLECTION
AVAILABLE TITLES

1. ENGLISH-SPANISH & SPANISH-ENGLISH
2. ENGLISH-ITALIAN & ITALIAN-ENGLISH
3. ENGLISH-FRENCH & FRENCH-ENGLISH
4. ENGLISH-GERMAN & GERMAN-ENGLISH
5. ENGLISH-PORTUGUESE & PORTUGUESE-ENGLISH
6. ENGLISH-CHINESE & CHINESE-ENGLISH
7. ENGLISH-ARABIC & ARABIC-ENGLISH
8. ENGLISH-JAPANESE & JAPANESE-ENGLISH
9. ENGLISH-KOREAN & KOREAN-ENGLISH
10. ENGLISH-RUSSIAN & RUSSIAN-ENGLISH
11. ENGLISH-TURKISH & TURKISH-ENGLISH

GET THE AUDIOVISUAL AND
INTERACTIVE CONTENT AT
QuickLanguages.com

LEARN MORE ABOUT OUR BOOKS AT:
americanbookgroup.com

AMERICAN
BOOK GROUP

COMPANION ONLINE COURSE
quicklanguages.com

Quick Languages: 1,000 Key Words and Expressions Phrasebook
ENGLISH-TURKISH & TURKISH-ENGLISH

To request permissions, contact the publisher at info@trialtea.com

Paperback ISBN: 978-1-681656-18-2

Library of Congress Control Code: 2023932195

First paperback edition: April 2023

Edited by Gregorio García
Cover art by Natalia Urbano
Layout by Esmeralda Riveros & Pancho Guijarro

Printed in the USA

American Book Group
americanbookgroup.com

Quick Languages / 1,000 Key Words and Phrases

INDEX OF CONTENTS

1,000 KEY WORDS AND EXPRESSIONS

English / Turkish - Turkish / English

Keep practicing at:
QuickLanguages.com

1. Greetings / Selam

Hi! / Hello!	Merhaba / Selam!
Good morning	Günaydın!
Good afternoon	İyi günler!
Good evening / Good night	İyi akşamlar! / İyi geceler!
How are you doing?	Nasılsın?
Fine	İyi
Very well	Pek iyi
Thank you / Thanks	Teşekkür ederim / Teşekkürler
Thank you very much	Çok teşekkür
You're welcome	Rica ederim
Fine, thank you	İyi, sağ ol
And you?	Ya sen?
See you	Görüşmek üzere!
See you later	Görüşürüz!
See you tomorrow	Yarın görüşürüz!
Goodbye	Allahaısmarladık
Bye	Güle güle!

2. Introductions and Courtesy Expressions / Tanışma ve nezaket deyimleri

What is your name?	**Adınız ne?**
My name is ...	**Adım ...**
Who are you?	**Siz kimsiniz?**
I am ...	**Ben ...**
Who is he / she?	**Bu efendi kimdir?/Bu bayan kimdir?**
He is ... / She is ...	**Bu efendi ... / Bu bayan ...**
Nice to meet you / Pleased to meet you	**Tanıştığımızdan memnun oldum**
Nice to meet you, too	**Ben de memnun oldum**
It's my pleasure	**Memnuniyet benim**
Excuse me	**Özür dilerim / Affedersiniz**
Please	**Lütfen / Efendim**
One moment, please	**Bir an, lütfen**
Welcome	**Hoş geldin!**
Go ahead	**Buyurunuz**
Can you repeat, please?	**Tekrar söyler misiniz, lütfen?**
I don't understand	**Anlayamam**
I understand a little	**Biraz anlıyorum**
Can you speak more slowly, please?	**Daha yavaş konuşabilir misiniz, lütfen?**
Do you speak Spanish?	**İspanyolca biliyor musunuz?**
How do you say hello in Spanish?	**Merhaba kelimesinin İspanyolca'sı nasıl?**
What does it mean?	**Bu ne demek?**
I speak Spanish a little	**Biraz İspanyolca biliyorum**

3. Ways to Address to a Person / Bir kimseye hitap kelimeleri

Madam / Ma'am	Bayan / Bayan efendi
Miss	Bayan
Ms.	Bayan
Mr.	Efendi / Beyefendi / Bay / Bey
Mrs.	Bayan / Bayan efendi
Sir	Efendi / Beyefendi
Dr.	Doktor

4. The Articles / Yoktur

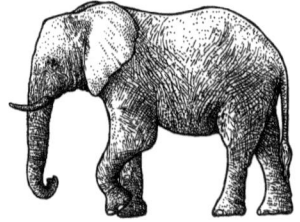

The	∅
The car	araba
The cars	arabalar
The house	ev
The houses	evler
A	bir
A car	bir araba
A house	bir ev
An	bir
An elephant	bir fil
An apple	bir elma
Some	birkaç
Some cars	birkaç araba / birkaç arabalar
Some houses	birkaç ev / birkaç evler

5. The Subject Pronouns
/ Şahıs zamirleri

I	**Ben**
You	**Sen**
He	**O**
She	**O**
It	**O**
We	**Biz**
You	**Siz**
They	**Onlar**

6. The Possessive Adjectives
/ İyelik zamirleri

My	**Benim**
Your	**Senin**
His	**Onun**
Her	**Onun**
Its	**Onun**
Our	**Bizim**
Your	**Sizin**
Their	**Onların**
My car	**(Benim) arabam**
Your book	**(Senin) kitabın**
His TV	**(Onun) televizyonu**
Our house	**(Bizim) evimiz**

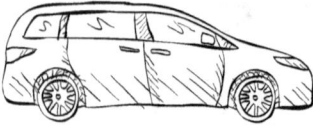

7. The Demonstrative Adjectives / İşaret zamirleri

This	**Bu**
This book	**Bu kitap**
This shirt	**Bu gömlek**
These	**Bunlar**
These books	**Bu kitaplar**
These shirts	**Bu gömlekler**
That	**Şu**
That table	**Şu masa**
That car	**Şu araba**
Those	**Şunlar**
Those tables	**Şu masalar**
Those cars	**Şu arabalar**

8. The Possessive Pronouns / İyelik zamirleri

Mine	**Benim**
Yours	**Senin**
His	**Onun**
Hers	**Onun**
Its	**Onun**
Ours	**Bizim**
Yours	**Sizin**
Theirs	**Onların**
The car is mine	**Araba benim**
The book is yours	**Kitap senin**
That TV is his	**Bu televizyon onundur**
This house is ours	**Bu ev bizim**

9. The Cardinal Numbers
/ Sayı sıfatları

0 / Zero	**Sıfır**
1 / One	**Bir**
2 / Two	**İki**
3 / Three	**Üç**
4 / Four	**Dört**
5 / Five	**Beş**
6 / Six	**Altı**
7 / Seven	**Yedi**
8 / Eight	**Sekiz**
9 / Nine	**Dokuz**
10 / Ten	**On**
11 / Eleven	**On bir**
12 / Twelve	**On iki**
13 / Thirteen	**On üç**
14 / Fourteen	**On dört**
15 / Fifteen	**On beş**
16 / Sixteen	**On altı**
17 / Seventeen	**On yedi**
18 / Eighteen	**On sekiz**
19 / Nineteen	**On dokuz**
20 / Twenty	**Yirmi**
21 / Twenty-one	**Yirmi bir**
30 / Thirty	**Otuz**
40 / Forty	**Kırk**
50 / Fifty	**Elli**
60 / Sixty	**Altmış**

1. 2. 3. 4.
5. 6. 7. 8.
9. 0.

9. The Cardinal Numbers
/ Sayı sıfatları

70 / Seventy	Yetmiş
80 / Eighty	Seksen
90 / Ninety	Doksan
100 / One hundred	Yüz
101 / One hundred and one	Yüz bir
200 / Two hundred	İki yüz
300 / Three hundred	Üç yüz
400 / Four hundred	Dört yüz
500 / Five hundred	Beş yüz
600 / Six hundred	Altı yüz
700 / Seven hundred	Yedi yüz
800 / Eight hundred	Sekiz yüz
900 / Nine hundred	Dokuz yüz
1,000 / One thousand	Bin
10,000 / Ten thousand	On bin
100,000 / One hundred thousand	Yüz bin
1,000,000 / One million	Bir milyon
1,000,000,000 / One billion	Bir milyar
Forty-five (45)	Kırk beş
One hundred and twenty-eight (128)	Yüz yirmi sekiz
One thousand nine hundred and sixty-three (1,963)	Bin dokuz yüz altmış üç
Six thousand and thirty-seven (6,037)	Altı bin otuz yedi
Eleven thousand (11,000)	On bir bin
Two hundred and seventy-nine thousand (279,000)	İki yüz yetmiş dokuz bin
Two million (2,000,000)	İki milyon

10. The Time
/ Saat

The clock	**Saat (duvar saati)**
The watch	**Saat (el saati)**
What time is it?	**Saat kaç?**
It is ...	**Saat ...**
It is one o'clock (1:00)	**Saat bir (1:00)**
It is two o'clock (2:00)	**Saat iki (2:00)**
It is three fifteen / It is a quarter past three (3:15)	**Saat üç çeyrek / Saat üçü on beş geçiyor (3:15)**
It is four thirty / It is half past four (4:30)	**Saat dört buçuk (4:30)**
It is five forty-five / It is a quarter to six (5:45)	**Saat beş kırk beş / Saat altıya on beş var (5:45)**
It is six fifty / It is ten to seven (6:50)	**Saat altı elli / Saat yediye on kalıyor (6:50)**
It is noon (12:00 P. M.)	**Öğle vakti (12:00)**
It is midnight (12:00 A. M.)	**Gece yarısı (00:00)**
In the morning	**Sabah**
In the afternoon	**Öğleden sonra**
In the evening	**Akşam**
At night	**Gece**
At what time is ...?	**Saat kaçta ...?**
At what time is the concert?	**Konser saat kaçta başlıyor ?**
At ...	**Saat ...**
At 7:10 P.M. (seven ten in the evening)	**Saat 7:10 (saat yediyi on geçe)**

11. The Days of the Week / **Hafta günleri**

Monday	**Pazartesi**
Tuesday	**Salı**
Wednesday	**Çarşamba**
Thursday	**Perşembe**
Friday	**Cuma**
Saturday	**Cumartesi**
Sunday	**Pazar**
What day is today?	**Bugün günlerden hangi gün?**

12. The Months of the Year / **Yılın ayları**

January	**Ocak**
February	**Şubat**
March	**Mart**
April	**Nisan**
May	**Mayıs**
June	**Haziran**
July	**Temmuz**
August	**Ağustos**
September	**Eylül**
October	**Ekim**
November	**Kasım**
December	**Aralık**
What is today's date?	**Bugün ayın kaçı?**

13. The Weather
/ Hava

English	Turkish
Sunny	**Güneşli**
Cloudy	**Bulutlu**
Rainy	**Yağmurlu**
Humid	**Nemli**
Dry	**Kuru**
Cold	**Soğuk**
Warm	**Sıcak**
Hot	**Çok sıcak**
Rain	**Yağmur**
Snow	**Kar**
How is the weather today?	**Bugün hava nasıl?**
It's nice	**Hava güzel**
It's sunny	**Güneşli**
It's cold in winter	**Kışın hava soğuk**
It's raining	**Yağmur yağıyor**
It's snowing	**Kar yağıyor**
I am cold	**Üşüyorum**

14. The Seasons
/ Mevsimler

Spring	İlk bahar
Summer	Yaz
Fall	Son bahar
Winter	Kış

15. The Colors
/ Renkler

Yellow	Sarı
Red	Kırmızı
Blue	Mavi
Green	Yeşil
Orange	Turuncu
Brown	Kahverengi
Pink	Pembe
Purple	Mor
Black	Siyah
White	Beyaz
Gray	Gri
Light	Açık
Dark	Koyu
Light green	Açık yeşil
Orange book	Portakal renkli kitap
Brown shoes	Kahverengi ayakkabı
My blouse is white	Bluzum beyaz
What color is...?	....rengi ne? / Hangi renk?
What is your favorite color?	En çok sevdiğin renk hangisi? / En sevdiğin renk ne?

16. The Parts of the Face / Yüz

Cheek	**Yanak**
Chin	**Çene**
Ear	**Kulak**
Eye	**Göz**
Forehead	**Alın**
Hair	**Saç**
Lips	**Dudak**
Mouth	**Ağız**
Nose	**Burun**
Skin	**Cilt**
Teeth	**Dişler**
Tooth	**Diş**
Blond / Blonde	**Sarı/ sarşın / sarı saçlı**
Brown	**Kumral**
Gray	**Kır saçlı**
Red hair	**Kızıl saçlı / kırmızı saçlı**
Long	**Uzun saçlı**
Short	**Kısa saçlı**
Straight	**Düz saçlı**
Curly	**Kıvırcık saçlı**
John is blond	**John sarı / John sarı saçlı**
Karen has long hair	**Karen uzun saçlı**
He has green eyes	**O yeşil gözlü**
Her eyes are blue	**O mavi gözlü bayan**
His eyes are big and brown	**Gözleri iri ve kahverengi**

17. Essential Verbs / **Esas fiiller**

Be	**Olmak**
Go	**Gitmek**
Come	**Gelmek**
Have	**Sahip olmak**
Get	**Almak**
Help	**Yardım etmek**
Love	**Sevmek**
Like	**Beğenmek**
Want	**İstemek**
Buy	**Satın almak**
Sell	**Satmak**
Read	**Okumak**
Write	**Yazmak**
Drink	**İçmek**
Eat	**Yemek**
Open	**Açmak**
Close	**Kapatmak**
Look at	**Bakmak**
Look for	**Aramak**
Find	**Bulmak**
Start	**Başlamak**
Stop	**Birakmak**
Pull	**Çekmek**

17. Essential Verbs
/ Esas fiiller

Push	**İtmek**
Send	**Göndermek**
Receive	**Almak**
Turn on	**Açmak**
Turn off	**Söndürmek**
Listen to	**Dinlemek**
Speak	**Konuşmak**
Do	**Yapmak**
Drive	**Araba kullanmak (sürmek)**
Feel	**Hissetmek**
Know	**Bilmek**
Leave	**Terk etmek, çıkmak**
Live	**Yaşamak**
Make	**Hazırlamak**
Meet	**Tanışmak**
Need	**İhtiyacı olmak / Muhtaç olmak**
Pay	**Ödemek**
Play	**Oynamak**
Remember	**Hatırlamak**
Repeat	**Tekrarlamak**
Say	**Söylemek**
Sit	**Oturmak**
Sleep	**Uyumak**

17. Essential Verbs / Esas fiiller

Study	**Öğrenmek**
Take	**Almak**
Think	**Düşünmek**
Understand	**Anlamak**
Wait	**Beklemek**
Watch	**İzlemek**
There is	**Var/Bulunuyor**
There are	**Var/Bulunuyor**
I am tall	**Ben uzun boyluyum**
You are short	**Sen kısa boylusun**
He is thin	**O zayıf.**
We are big	**Biz büyüküz**
They are intelligent	**Onlar akıllıdırlar**
I am at home	**Ben evdeyim**
You are at school	**Sen okuldasın**
We are at the store	**Biz mağazadayız**
I get a prize	**(Ben bir) ödül kazanıyorum**
I go to the movies	**Sinemaya gidiyorum**
I have a nice car	**Benim güzel bir arabam var**
I listen to the music	**Müzik dinliyorum**
I watch TV.	**Televizyon izliyorum**
I like this book	**Bu kitabı beğeniyorum**
There are ten children in the park	**Parkta on çocuk var**

18. Interrogative Words
/ Soru zamirleri

How many ...?	**Kaç ....?**
How much...?	**Ne kadar ....?**
How ...?	**Nasıl...?**
What ...?	**Ne...?**
When ...?	**Ne zaman...?**
Where ...?	**Nerede/Nereye/Nereden...?**
Which ...?	**Hangi...?**
Who ...?	**Kim...?**
Whose ...?	**Kimin...?**
Whom ...? / To whom ...?	**Kimi...? / Kime ...?**
Why ...?	**Neden/Niçin...?**
Because ...	**Çünkü....**

19. Linking Words
/ Bağlaçlar

And	**ve / ile**
But	**ama / fakat**
Or	**veya / yoksa**
Either ... or	**gerek ... gerek**
Neither ... nor	**ne ... ne**
Yes	**Evet**
No	**Hayır**
So	**o halde / demek ki/yani**
While	**zaman / süre / ...esnasında**

20. The Prepositions / Edatlar

About	**hakkında**
Above	**üzerinde**
Across	**karşı/karşısında**
At	**-da, '-de, '-a, '-e, '-ya, '-ye**
Behind	**arakada / arkasında / -in arkasinda**
Below	**altında**
Between	**arasında**
By	**ile**
Down	**aşağıda**
During	**.... zamanında / ... esnasında / ... sırasında**
For	**için**
From	**-den**
In	**içinde**
In front of	**önünde**
Into	**içinde**

20. The Prepositions / Edatlar

Near	**yakında**
Next to	**yanında**
Of	**_l, _in, _un, ün....**
On	**üstünde/üzerinde**
Out	**dışarıda**
Over	**üstünde/üzerinde**
Per	**başına/her biri için**
Through	**-den**
To	**doğru**
Under	**altında**
Up	**yukarıya**
With	**ile**
Without	**-siz, '-sız, '-suz, '-süz**
The cat is in the box	**Kedi kutunun içindedir**
The vase is on the table	**Vazo masanın üstündedir**
Somebody is at the door	**Biri kapının önündedir**

21. Giving Directions
/ Yön göstermek /
Talimat vermek

At the corner	**Köşede**
Far	**-den uzak**
Near	**-ye yakın**
Go straight ahead	**Doğru / düz gidiniz**
Left	**Sola**
Right	**Sağa**
Turn left	**Sola çeviriniz**
Turn right	**Sağa çeviriniz**
Go straight one block	**Bundan sonraki sokağa kadar doğruya devam ediniz**
After the traffic light, turn right	**Trafik ışığından sonra sağa çeviriniz**
How can I get to ...?	**-ye nasıl ulaşabilirim / gidebilirim?**
Where is the ...?	**... Nerede bulunuyor?**
Where is the church?	**Kilise nerede bulunuyor ? / Kilise nerede?**
The museum is next to the shopping center	**Müze alış-veriş merkezinin yanında bulunuyor**
The drugstore is in front of the building	**Eczane binanın karşısında bulunuyor**
The supermarket is near the park	**Süpermarket parkın yakınındadır**

22. The Ordinal Numbers
/ Sıra sayıları

English	Turkish
First	**Birinci**
Second	**İkinci**
Third	**Üçüncü**
Fourth	**Dördüncü**
Fifth	**Beşinci**
Sixth	**Altıncı**
Seventh	**Yedinci**
Eighth	**Sekizinci**
Ninth	**Dokuzuncu**
Tenth	**Onuncu**
Eleventh	**On birinci**
Twelfth	**On ikinci**
Twentieth	**Yirminci**
Thirtieth	**Otuzuncu**
The first building	**Birinci bina**
The second floor	**İkinci kat**

23. Countries, Nationalities, and Languages / Devletler, uyrukluk ve diller

Brazil (Country)	**Brezilya**
Brazilian (Nationality)	**Brezilyalı**
Portuguese (Language)	**Portekizce**
Colombia	**Kolombiya**
Colombian	**Kolombiya'lı**
Spanish	**İspanyolca**
China	**Çin**
Chinese	**Çin**
Chinese	**Çince**
England	**İngiltere**
English	**İngiliz**
English	**İngilizce**
France	**Fransa**
French	**Fransız**
French	**Fransızca**
Germany	**Almanya**
German	**Alman**
German	**Almanca**
Italy	**İtalya**

23. Countries, Nationalities, and Languages /
Devletler, uyrukluk ve diller

Italian	İtalyan/İtalyalı
Italian	İtalyanca
Japan	Japonya
Japanese	Japon/Japonyalı
Japanese	Japonca
Mexico	Meksika
Mexican	Meksikalı
Spanish	İspanyolca
Spain	İspanya
Spanish	İspanyol
Spanish	İspanyolca
United States of America (U.S.A.)	Amerika Birleşik Devletleri (ABD)
American	Amerikan / Amerikalı
English	İngilizce
Where are you from?	Nerelisiniz?
I am from Brazil	Brezilya'dan geliyorum
I am Brazilian	Ben brezilyalıyım / Ben brezilyanım
I speak Portuguese	Portekizce biliyorum
I am not from Italy	Ben italyan değilim

24. Indefinite Pronouns / Belirsiz zamirler

Anybody	**kimse, hiç kimse**
Anything	**bir şey**
Nobody	**hiç kimse**
Nothing	**hiçbir şey**
Somebody	**biri (si)**
Something	**bir şey**
Everybody	**herkes**
Everything	**her şey**
Is anybody home?	**Evde biri (si) var mı?**
I don't want anything	**Bir şey istemem / Bir şey istemiyorum**
Nothing happened	**Hiç bir şey olmadı**
Somebody is in the living room	**Salonda biri (si) var**
Everything is ready	**Her şey hazır**

25. The Emotions / Duygu

English	Turkish
Angry	Öfkeli, kızgın
Bored	Bıkkın
Confident	Kendinden emin
Confused	Şaşkın / karışık / şaşırmış
Embarrassed	Utangaç
Excited	Heyecanlı
Happy	Neşeli
Nervous	Sinirli
Proud	Gururlu
Sad	Üzgün
Scared	Korkak
Shy	Utangaç / Çekingen
Surprised	Şaşkın / Hayret içinde
Worried	Endişeli
I am happy	Ben memnunum / mutluyum
He is sad	O üzüntülü
They are surprised	(Onlar) Şaşkındırlar
Are you excited?	Sen heyecanlandın mı?
I am not bored	Bıkkın değilim
She is not nervous	(o) Sinirli değil
Everybody is confident	Kerkes kendine emin

26. Adverbs
/ Zarflar

A few	**birkaç**
A little	**az**
A lot	**çok**
After	**sonra**
Again	**tekrar**
Ago	**önce**
Also	**yine**
Always	**daima/ her zaman**
Before	**önce**
Enough	**yeter**
Everyday	**her gün**
Exactly	**tam / doğru**
Finally	**eninde sonunda**
First	**ilk önce**
Here	**burada**
Late	**geç**
Later	**daha sonra**
Never	**hiçbir zaman**
Next	**bundan sonraki**
Now	**şimdi**

26. Adverbs
/ Zarflar

Often	çoğu zaman
Once	bir kez
Only	yalnız / sadece
Outside	dışarıda
Really	Sahi / gerçekten / sahiden
Right here	tam bu yerde
Right now	hemen
Since	o zamandan beri
Slowly	yavaş
Sometimes	ara sıra / bazen
Soon	yakinda
Still	henüz
Then	o zaman / ondan sonra
There	orada
Today	bugün
Tomorrow	yarın
Tonight	bu akşam
Too	da/de
Usually	genellikle

27. Auxiliary Verbs / Yardımcı fiiller

Can	**bilmek**
Could	**olabilir**
Did	**olmak, sahip olmak**
Do	**∅**
Does	**olmak**
Have to	**-meye mecbur olmak, mecbur**
May	**-ebilmek**
Must	**-meli**
Should	**-meli**
Will	**olmak, -ecek**
Would	**Olur**
Can you go to the movies?	**Sinemaya gelebilir (gidebilirmisin) misin?**
Could I have change?	**Para bozdurabilir misiniz?**
Did you work at the drugstore?	**Eczanede mi çalışmıştın?**
I did not (didn't) work at the drugstore	**Eczanede çalışmadım**
Do you work at the drugstore?	**Eczanede mi çalışıyorsun?**
I do not (don't) work at the drugstore	**Eczanede çalışmıyorum**
Does he read the newspaper?	**(O) Gazeteyi okuyor mu?**
He does not (doesn't) read the newspaper	**(O) Gazeteyi okumuyor**
I have to do my homework	**Ev ödevimi yazmam gerek (lazım / yazmalıyım)**
May I help you?	**Sana yardım edebilir miyim?**
You must turn left now	**Şimdi sola çevirmen gerek (lazım / çevirmelisin)?**
You should go to the doctor	**Doktora gitmen gerek (lazım/gitmelisin)**
I will work tomorrow	**Yarın çalışacağım**
I would like a glass of wine	**Bir bardak şarap isterim**

28. Expressions
/ Deyimler

All right	**Peki**
Come in	**Buyurun/Buyurunuz**
Come here, please	**Buraya geliniz lütfen**
Don't worry!	**Sıkılma**
For example	**Örneğin / mesela**
Good luck!	**Bol şans dilerim!**
Great idea!	**Harika!**
Have a nice day!	**İyi günler!**
Help yourself!	**Buyurun!**
Here you are	**Buyurun!**
Hurry up!	**Acele et!**
I agree	**Kabul ediyorum**
I disagree	**Kabul etmiyorum**
I don't care	**Bu beni ilgilendirmez**
I don't know	**Bilmem**
I'm coming!	**Geliyorum**
I'm afraid...	**-den korkuyorum**
It's a deal!	**Tamam! / Oldu!**
Keep well!	**Kendine bak!**
Let me think	**Biraz düşüneyim**
Let's go!	**Gidelim!**
Right now	**Hemen / şimdi / derhal**
Sounds good!	**Pek iyi!**
Sure	**Muhakkak**
Take a seat	**Buyurun, oturunuz**
Take care!	**Kendine iyi bak!**

29. The Family
/ Aile

Father	**Baba**
Mother	**Anne**
Son	**Oğul**
Daughter	**Kız**
Brother	**Kardeş**
Sister	**Kız kardeşi**
Grandfather	**Dede**
Grandmother	**Büyük anne / anneanne**
Uncle	**Amca**
Aunt	**Hala**
Cousin	**Kuzin / kuzen**
Nephew	**Yeğen**
Niece	**Kardeş kızı (kiz) yeğen**
Husband	**Eş, koca**
Wife	**Eş, karı**
Boyfriend	**Nişanlı / arkadaş**
Girlfriend	**Nişanlı, kız arkadaşı**
In-laws	**Dünür**
Father in-law	**Kaynata (kayınpeder)**
Mother in-law	**Kaynana (kayınvalide)**
Brother in-law	**Kayınbirader / enişte / bacanak**
Sister in-law	**Görümce / baldız / elti / yenge**
Step father	**Üvey baba / babalık**
Step mother	**Üvey ana / analık**
Step brother	**Üvey kardeş**
Step sister	**Üvey kız kardeş**
Who is he?	**O kimdir?**
He is my brother	**O kardeşimdir**

30. The House
/ Ev

English	Turkish
Living room	**Oturma odası**
Door	**Kapı**
Window	**Pencere**
Sofa	**Kanepe**
Lamp	**Lamba**
Dining room	**Yemek odası**
Table	**Masa**
Chair	**İskemle, sandalye**
Kitchen	**Mutfak**
Stove	**Soba**
Oven	**Fırın**
Fridge	**Buzdolabı**
Microwave	**Mikrodalga sobası**
Bedroom	**Yatak odası**
Bed	**Yatak**
Nightstand	**Komodin**
Vanity	**Tuvalet masası**
Chest of drawers	**Komot**
Closet	**Dolap**
Bathroom	**Banyo**
Mirror	**Ayna**
Sink	**Lavabo**
Toilet	**Tuvalet**
Bathtub	**Küvet**
Laundry room	**Çamaşırhane**
Driveway	**Park yeri**
Where is the living room?	**Oturma odası nerede?**
The door is big	**Kapı büyük**
The stove is small	**Soba küçük**
The kitchen is beautiful	**Mutfak güzel**

31. The City
/ Şehir

Block	**Semt**
Building	**Bina**
Church	**Kilise**
Movie theater	**Sinema**
Museum	**Müze**
Park	**Park**
Drugstore	**Eczane**
Restaurant	**Lokanta**
Shopping center	**Alış-veriş merkezi**
Store	**Mağaza**
Street	**Sokak, cadde**
Supermarket	**Süpermarket**

32. At the Supermarket / Mağazada

English	Turkish
The food	**Gıda**
The fruits	**Meyve**
Apple	**Elma**
Banana	**Muz**
Cherry	**Kiraz**
Grapes	**Üzüm**
Orange	**Portakal**
Strawberry	**Çilek**
The vegetables	**Sebze**
Beans	**Fasulye**
Carrot	**Havuç**
Cauliflower	**Karnabahar**
Lettuce	**Salata / marul**
Onion	**Soğan**
Pepper	**Biber**
Potato	**Patates**
Tomato	**Domates**
The meats	**Et**
Beef	**Dana eti**
Chicken	**Piliç / tavuk eti**
Turkey	**Hindi**
Ham	**Jambon**
Pork	**Domuz eti**
The dairy products	**Süt ürünleri**
Butter	**Tereyağı**
Cheese	**Peynir**
Milk	**Süt**

32. At the Supermarket / Mağazada

Yogurt	**Yoğurt**
Jam	**Reçel**
Bread	**Ekmek**
Eggs	**Yumurta**
Fish	**Balık**
Seafood	**Deniz hayvanları**
Can	**Konserve**
Cart	**Pazar arabası**
Bag	**Torba**
Basket	**Sepet**
Bottle	**Şişe**
Cash register	**Kasa**
Cashier	**Veznedar**
Customer service	**Müşteri hizmetleri**
Groceries	**Bakkaliye**
How many...?	**Kaç/ne kadar ....?**
How many oranges do you buy?	**Kaç portakal alıyorsunuz?**
How much does it cost?	**Fiyatı ne kadar?**
How much do the bananas cost?	**Muzlarin fıyatı kaç?**
I want...	**... istiyorum**
I want to buy a bottle of milk	**Bir şişe süt almak istiyorum**
I would like...	**... isterim**
I would like a bag of tomatoes	**1 poşet domates almak istiyorum**
Where is the lettuce?	**Yeşil salata nerede?**
It's on aisle one	**Birinci sırada**
Where are the cans of vegetables?	**Sebze konserveleri nerede?**
They are on aisle five	**Beşinci sırada**

33. At the Restaurant
/ Lokantada

Waiter / waitress	Garson
Breakfast	Kahvaltı
Lunch	Öğle yemeği
Dinner	Akşam yemeği
To eat	Yemek
To drink	İçmek
To eat breakfast	Kahvaltı yapmak
The menu	Yemek listesi/ menü
Appetizer	Meze
Salad	Salata
Soup	Çorba
Main course	Yemek
Pasta	Makarna
Rice	Pirinç
French fries	Kızartılmış patates
Mashed potatoes	Patates ezmesi
Baked potatoes	Patates kızartması
Barbecue	Izgara
Fried chicken	Piliç kızartması
Steak	Pirzola

33. At the Restaurant / Lokantada

English	Turkish
Dessert	**Tatlı**
Beverages	**İçecekler**
Coffee	**Kahve**
Tea	**Çay**
Soda	**Gazoz**
Lemonade	**Limonata**
Orange juice	**Portakal suyu**
Alcoholic drinks	**Alkollü içkiler**
Beer	**Bira**
Wine	**Şarap**
Check	**Hesap**
Tip	**Bahşiş**
How may I help you?	**Size yardım edebilir miyim?**
What would you like to order?	**Siparişinizi alabilir miyim?**
May I have the menu, please?	**Yemek listesini verir misiniz, lütfen?**
Could I get more water, please?	**Biraz su getiri misiniz, lütfen?**
My order is wrong	**Bunu ısmarlamış değilim**
The service here is wonderful!	**Burada hizmet çok iyi**
The food is delicious!	**Yemek çok lezzetli**
The check, please	**Hesap lütfen**
The tip is included	**Bahşiş dahil**

34. The Office
/ Ofiste

Book	**Kitap**
Calculator	**Hesap makinesi**
Computer	**Bilgisayar**
Desk	**Büro**
Fax machine	**Faks makinesi**
File	**Dosya**
File cabinet	**Dosya dolabı**
Folder	**Dosya**
Keyboard	**Klavye**
Monitor	**Monitör**
Mouse	**Fare**
Notebook	**Karne**
Pad	**Fare altlığı**
Paper	**Kağıt**
Pen	**Tükenmez**
Printer	**Yazıcı**
Ruler	**Cetvel**
Scissors	**Makas**
Screen	**Ekran**
Stapler	**Tel zımba**
Telephone	**Telefon**
My computer is broken	**Bilgisayarım arızalı**
There is no paper in the printer	**Yazıcıda kağıt yok**
We need to buy more folders	**Daha çok dosya almamız gerek**
We don't have a copy machine	**Kopya makinemiz yok**

35. Jobs and Positions
/ Meslek ve görevler

Accountant	**Muhasebeci**
Architect	**Mimar**
Artist	**Artist**
Chef	**Baş aşçı**
Clerk	**Memur / görevli**
Cook	**Aşçı**
Doctor	**Doktor**
Engineer	**Mühendis**
Gardener	**Bahçıvan**
Graphic designer	**Dizayner / tasarımcı**
Lawyer	**Avukat**
Nurse	**Hemşire**
Physician	**Hekim**
Salesperson	**Satıcı**
Secretary	**Sekreter**
Security guard	**Koruma memuru**
Taxi driver	**Taksi sürücüsü**
Teacher	**Öğretmen**
Technician	**Teknisyen**
Tourist guide	**Rehber**
Travel agent	**Turizm acentesi**

1,000 Key Words and Phrases

36. Job Interview
/ İş başvurusu

Apply for a job	**İş arama**
Duty	**Pozisyon**
Experience	**Tecrübe**
Last name	**Soyadı**
First name	**Ad**
Full time job	**Tam mesai saatler**
Part time job	**Saatlik iş**
Résumé	**Özgeçmiş**
Skill	**Yetenekler**
Work	**Çalışmak / iş**

37. The Transportation
/ Taşıt araçları

Airplane	**Uçak**
Bicycle	**Bisiklet**
Bus	**Otobüs**
Car	**Oto/araba**
Helicopter	**Helikopter**
Metro	**Metro**
Motorcycle	**Motosiklet**
Train	**Tren**
Truck	**Kamyon**

38. The Traffic / Ulaştırma

Bus stop	Otobüs durağı
Crosswalk	Yaya geçidi
Freeway, highway	Otoyol
Gas station	Benzin istasyonu
Intersection	Kavşak
Lane	Yol şeridi
No outlet	Çıkmaz yol
One way	Tek istikametli yol
Pedestrian	Yaya
Speed	Sürat/Hız
Stop sign	Stop
To get in	Binmek
To get off	İnmek
Toll	Yol ücreti
Traffic light	Trafik ışıkları
Train station	Istasyon
Two way	İki istikametli yol
U-turn	Dönüş
Yield	Yer vermek
I get in the car	Arabaya binmek
I get off the car	Arabadan inmek
We wait for the train	Treni bekliyoruz

39. The Car
/ Otomobil/araba

Accelerator	**Gaz pedalı**
Battery	**Akü**
Hood	**Motor kapağı**
Brake	**Fren**
Clutch	**Debriyaj**
Engine	**Motor**
Fender	**Tampon**
Gear box	**Vites kutusu**
Headlight	**Far**
Rear view mirror	**Ayna**
Make	**Marka**
Model	**Model**
Radiator	**Radyatör**
Steering wheel	**Direksiyon simidi**
Seat	**Koltuk**
Tire	**Lastik**
Trunk	**Bagaj**
Wheel	**Tekerlek**
Windshield	**Ön cam**
Windshield wipers	**Ön cam siperi**
The car is broken	**Araba arızalandı**
I have a flat tire	**Lastik patladı**
I need a new battery	**Yeni aküye ihtiyacım var**
What year is the car?	**Otonun imalat yılı hangisi?**
What make is the car?	**Otonun markası ne?**
What model is the car?	**Otonun modeli ne?**
How many miles does the car have?	**Otomobilin kaç kilometresi var?**

40. Phone Conversations / Ttelefon görüşmesi

Call	Telefon etmek
Dial	Çevirmek
Directory	Telefon rehberi
Directory Assistance	Enformasyon
Extension	Uzatma numarası
Hold on, please	Bir saniye, lütfen
I'd like to speak to...	.... İle görüşebilir miyim
I'll put you through	Bağlıyorum
I'll transfer your call	Görüşmenizi İletiyorum
I'm calling about ...	.... İle ilgili olarak telefon ediyorum
Just a minute	Biraz bekler misiniz, lütfen
Leave a message	Mesajınız olacak mı?
Let me see...	Bakayım ....
Phone	Telefonla aramak
Phone number	Telefon numarası
Ring	Telefon etmek
Speak	Seslenmek
Speaking	Telefonda ....
Take a message	Mesaj iletmek
Talk	Konuşmak
This is...	Telefonda ....
Who's calling?	Kiminle görüşüyorum?

41. At the Post Office
/ Postada

English	Turkish
Air mail	**Uçak postası**
Counter	**Gişe**
Envelope	**Zarf**
Letter	**Mektup**
Mail	**Yazışma**
Parcel	**Koli**
Postcard	**Kart postal**
Postman, mailman	**Postacı**
Stamp	**Posta pulu / pul**
To send	**Göndermek**
To deliver	**Sevk etmek / teslim etmek / temin etmek**
Delivery	**Sevk**
To pick up	**Almak**
Address	**Adres**
I want to send a letter	**Mektup göndermek istiyorum.**
I would like to pick up a parcel	**Bir koli (paket) almak istiyorum.**
How much do the stamps cost?	**Pulların fiyatı ne kadar?**
Do you sell postcards?	**Kart postal(lar) satıyor musunuz?**

42. At the Bank
/ Bankada

Account	**Hesap**
ATM	**Bankamatik / paramatik**
Bank statement	**Banka beyanı**
Bank teller	**Veznedar / kasiyer**
Cash	**Nakit para**
Checkbook	**Çek defteri**
Checking account	**Cari hesap**
Credit card	**Kredi kartı**
Debit card	**Zimmet kartı**
Deposit slip	**Depozito bordrosu / ödeme belgesi**
Savings account	**Tasarruf hesabı**
To deposit	**Yatırmak**
To save	**Tasarruf etmek**
To transfer	**Havale etmek**
To withdraw	**Çekmek**
Transactions	**Banka işlemi**
Withdrawal slip	**Çekme bordrosu**
I want to make a deposit	**Depozito hesabı açtırmak istiyorum**
Do you have a savings account?	**Tasarruf hesabınız var mı?**
I have a checking account	**Cari hesabım var**
What is your credit card number?	**Kredi kartınızın numarası ne?**
I don't have an ATM card	**Bankamatik kartım yok?**
Where are the deposit slips?	**Depozito tahsil senetleri nerede?**

43. At the Airport
/ Hava limanında

English	Turkish
Arrival	**Varış**
Concourse	**Bekleme salonu**
Customs	**Gümrük**
Departure	**Kalkış**
Destination	**Gidilecek yer / yolculuk hedefi**
Entrance	**Giriş**
Exit	**Çıkış**
First class	**Birinci mevki**
Flight	**Uçuş**
Gate	**Terminal**
Immigrations office	**İltica Şubesi**
Luggage	**Bagaj**
Passport	**Pasaport**
Restrooms	**Tuvalet**
Suitcase	**Valiz**
To arrive	**Varmak**
To depart	**Kalkmak**
To travel	**Yolculuk etmek / seyahat yapmak**
Trip	**Yolculuk / Seyahat**
Where are you traveling?	**Nereye yolculuk ediyorsunuz? / Yolculuk nereye?**
May I have your ticket, please?	**Biletinizi gösterir misiniz, lütfen?**
I need you passport, please	**Pasaportunuzu verir misiniz, lütfen**
My flight number is ...	**Uçuşun numarası ...**
Where is gate number ...?	**... Numaralı terminal nerede?**
The flight is delayed	**Uçuşun gecikmesi var**
The flight is on time	**Uçuş tam zamanında geliyor**

44. At the Hotel / Otelde

Double room	**İki kişilik oda**
Single room	**Tek kişilik oda**
Bell desk	**Resepsiyon**
Bellman	**Otel garsonu**
Elevator	**Asansör**
Reception	**Resepsiyon**
Receptionist	**Resepsiyon görevlisi**
Reservation	**Rezervasyon**
Stairway	**Merdiven**
Swimming pool	**Yüzme havuzu**
Tours desk	**Seyahat acentesi**
Valet parking	**Park etme hizmeti**
To check-in	**İşlem yapmak**
To check-out	**Otelden ayrılmak**
I would like to make a reservation	**Rezervasyon yapmak istiyorum**
I want a single room	**Tek kişilik oda istiyorum**
I would like to check-in	**Otele yerleşmek istiyorum**

45. The Clothes
/ Giyim

Bathing suit	**Mayo**
Belt	**Kemer**
Blouse	**Bluz**
Coat	**Palto**
Dress	**Elbise**
Gloves	**Eldiven**
Hat	**Şapka**
Jacket	**Ceket**
Pants	**Pantolon**
Purse	**Cüzdan / para kesesi**
Scarf	**Şal**
Shirt	**Gömlek**
Shoes	**Ayakkabı**
Shorts	**Şort**
Skirt	**Etek**
Socks	**Çorap**
Suit	**Takım**
Suitcase	**Valiz**
The size	**Boy**
Small	**Küçük**
Medium	**Orta**
Large	**Büyük**
Big sizes	**Büyük boy**

46. At the Shopping Center / Alış-veriş merkezinde

Department store	**Büyük mağaza**
Ladies	**Bayanlar**
Men	**Baylar**
Juniors	**Gençler**
Kids	**Çocuklar**
Ladies' department	**bayan giyimi**
Jewelry	**Mücevherat**
Fitting room	**Prova**
Elevator	**Asansör**
Escalator	**Yürüyen merdiven**
How may I help you?	**Yardım edebilir miyim?**
I'm looking for ...	**... arıyorum**
I'm just looking	**Yalnız bakıyorum ...**
Where is the fitting room?	**Prova odası nerede?**
It fits well	**Bana yakışıyor**
It doesn't fit well	**Bana yakışmıyor**
May I pay here?	**Burada ödeyebilir miyim?**
I want to exchange this	**Bunu değiştirmek istiyorum**
I want to return this	**Bunu geri vermek istiyorum**
I like ...	**Hoşuma gidiyor ...**
I like this blouse	**Bu bluz hoşuma gidiyor**
I don't like ...	**Hoşuma gitmiyor**
I don't like these pants	**Bu pantolon hoşuma gitmiyor**

47. At the Drugstore
/ Eczanede

Antiseptic	**Antiseptik / desinfektan (ilacı)**
Adhesive bandage	**Yara bandı**
Antibiotic	**Antibiyotik**
Aspirin	**Aspirin**
Bandage	**Sargı**
Cold medicine	**Soğuk alma ilacı**
Cough syrup	**Öksürük şurubu**
Medication	**İlaçlar**
Ointment	**Merhem**
OTC (Over The Counter) medication	**Reçetesiz ilaçlar**
Painkiller	**Ağrı kesici**
Pills	**Haplar**
Prescription	**Reçete**
Tablets	**Tabletler**
Thermometer	**Termometre**
Cotton	**Pamuk**

48. The Parts of the Body / Beden

Ankle	**Ayak bileği**
Arm	**Kol**
Back	**Sırt**
Buttock	**Kıç**
Calf	**Baldır**
Chest	**Göğüs**
Elbow	**Dirsek**
Feet	**Ayaklar**
Finger	**Parmak**
Foot	**Ayak**
Forearm	**Kol**
Hand	**El**
Head	**Baş**
Hip	**Kalça**
Knee	**Diz**
Leg	**Ayak**
Neck	**Boyun**
Shoulder	**Omuz**
Stomach	**Mide**
Thigh	**But**
Toe	**Ayak parmağı**
Waist	**Bel**
Wrist	**Bilek**

49. Health Problems
/ Sağlık problemleri

Backache	**Sırtım ağrıyor**
Cold	**Soğuk alma**
Fever	**Ateş**
Hurt	**Ağrımak / acımak**
Indigestion	**Mide bozukluğu**
Injury	**Yara**
Pain	**Ağrı**
Pulse	**Nabız**
Sick	**Hasta**
Sneeze	**Nezle**
Sore throat	**Boğaz ağrısı**
Toothache	**Diş ağrısı**
I have a headache	**Baş ağrısı**
I have a stomachache	**Mide ağrısı**
I have pain in my knee	**Dizim ağrıyor**
I hurt my hand	**Elimi yaraladım**
I've got a cold	**Üşütüm**
My foot hurts	**Ayağım ağrıyor**

50. The Animals
/ Hayvanlar

Bear	**Ayı**
Bird	**Kuş**
Cat	**Kedi**
Chicken	**Piliç**
Cow	**İnek**
Dog	**Köpek**
Duck	**Ördek**
Elephant	**Fil**
Fish	**Balık**
Horse	**At**
Lizard	**Kertenkele**
Lion	**Aslan**
Monkey	**Maymun**
Mouse	**Sıçan**
Rat	**Fare**
Tiger	**Kaplan**

EXERCISE!

Write the Turkish translation.

Keep practicing at:
QuickLanguages.com

1. Greetings
/ Selam

English	Turkish
Hi! / Hello!	Merhaba / Selam!
Good morning	
Good afternoon	
Good evening / Good night	
How are you doing?	
Fine	
Very well	
Thank you / Thanks	
Thank you very much	
You're welcome	
Fine, thank you	
And you?	
See you	
See you later	
See you tomorrow	
Goodbye	
Bye	

2. Introductions and Courtesy Expressions / Tanışma ve nezaket deyimleri

What is your name?

Adınız ne?

My name is ...

Who are you?

I am ...

Who is he / she?

He is ... / She is ...

Nice to meet you / Pleased to meet you

Nice to meet you, too

It's my pleasure

Excuse me

Please

One moment, please

Welcome

Go ahead

Can you repeat, please?

I don't understand

I understand a little

Can you speak more slowly, please?

Do you speak Spanish?

How do you say hello in Spanish?

What does it mean?

I speak Spanish a little

3. Ways to Address to a Person
/ Bir kimseye hitap kelimeleri

Madam / Ma'am	Bayan/Bayan efendi
Miss	
Ms.	
Mr.	
Mrs.	
Sir	
Dr.	

4. The Articles
/ Yoktur

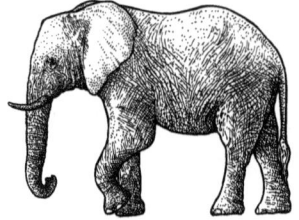

The	∅
The car	
The cars	
The house	
The houses	
A	
A car	
A house	
An	
An elephant	
An apple	
Some	
Some cars	
Some houses	

5. The Subject Pronouns
/ Şahıs zamirleri

I	Ben
You	
He	
She	
It	
We	
You	
They	

6. The Possessive Adjectives
/ İyelik zamirleri

My	Benim
Your	
His	
Her	
Its	
Our	
Your	
Their	
My car	
Your book	
His TV	
Our house	

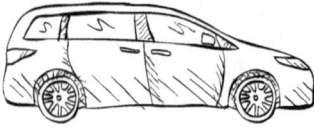

7. The Demonstrative Adjectives / İşaret zamirleri

This	Bu
This book	
This shirt	
These	
These books	
These shirts	
That	
That table	
That car	
Those	
Those tables	
Those cars	

8. The Possessive Pronouns / İyelik zamirleri

Mine	Benim
Yours	
His	
Hers	
Its	
Ours	
Yours	
Theirs	
The car is mine	
The book is yours	
That TV is his	
This house is ours	

9. The Cardinal Numbers
/ Sayı sıfatları

0 / Zero   Sıfır

1 / One

2 / Two

3 / Three

4 / Four

5 / Five

6 / Six

7 / Seven

8 / Eight

9 / Nine

10 / Ten

11 / Eleven

12 / Twelve

13 / Thirteen

14 / Fourteen

15 / Fifteen

16 / Sixteen

17 / Seventeen

18 / Eighteen

19 / Nineteen

20 / Twenty

21 / Twenty-one

30 / Thirty

40 / Forty

50 / Fifty

60 / Sixty

1. 2. 3. 4.
5. 6. 7. 8.
9. 0.

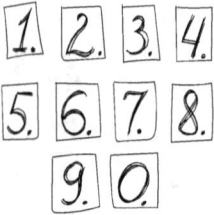

9. The Cardinal Numbers
/ Sayı sıfatları

70 / Seventy	Yetmiş
80 / Eighty	
90 /Ninety	
100 / One hundred	
101 / One hundred and one	
200 / Two hundred	
300 / Three hundred	
400 / Four hundred	
500 / Five hundred	
600 / Six hundred	
700 / Seven hundred	
800 / Eight hundred	
900 /Nine hundred	
1,000 / One thousand	
10,000 / Ten thousand	
100,000 / One hundred thousand	
1,000,000 / One million	
1,000,000,000 / One billion	
Forty-five (45)	
One hundred and twenty-eight (128)	
One thousand nine hundred and sixty-three (1,963)	
Six thousand and thirty-seven (6,037)	
Eleven thousand (11,000)	
Two hundred and seventy-nine thousand (279,000)	
Two million (2,000,000)	

10. The Time
/ Saat

The clock

Saat (duvar saati)

The watch

What time is it?

It is ...

It is one o'clock (1:00)

It is two o'clock (2:00)

It is three fifteen / It is a quarter past three (3:15)

It is four thirty / It is half past four (4:30)

It is five forty-five / It is a quarter to six (5:45)

It is six fifty / It is ten to seven (6:50)

It is noon (12:00 P. M.)

It is midnight (12:00 A. M.)

In the morning

In the afternoon

In the evening

At night

At what time is ...?

At what time is the concert?

At ...

At 7:10 P.M. (seven ten in the evening)

11. The Days of the Week
/ Hafta günleri

Monday	Pazartesi
Tuesday	
Wednesday	
Thursday	
Friday	
Saturday	
Sunday	
What day is today?	

12. The Months of the Year
/ Yılın ayları

January	Ocak
February	
March	
April	
May	
June	
July	
August	
September	
October	
November	
December	
What is today's date?	

13. The Weather
/ Hava

Sunny	*Güneşli*
Cloudy	
Rainy	
Humid	
Dry	
Cold	
Warm	
Hot	
Rain	
Snow	
How is the weather today?	
It's nice	
It's sunny	
It's cold in winter	
It's raining	
It's snowing	
I am cold	

14. The Seasons / Mevsimler

Spring	ilk bahar
Summer	
Fall	
Winter	

15. The Colors / Renkler

Yellow	Sarı
Red	
Blue	
Green	
Orange	
Brown	
Pink	
Purple	
Black	
White	
Gray	
Light	
Dark	
Light green	
Orange book	
Brown shoes	
My blouse is white	
What color is ...?	
What is your favorite color?	

16. The Parts of the Face
/ Yüz

Yanak

Cheek

Chin

Ear

Eye

Forehead

Hair

Lips

Mouth

Nose

Skin

Teeth

Tooth

Blond / Blonde

Brown

Gray

Red hair

Long

Short

Straight

Curly

John is blond

Karen has long hair

He has green eyes

Her eyes are blue

His eyes are big and brown

17. Essential Verbs
/ Esas fiiller

Be	Olmak
Go	
Come	
Have	
Get	
Help	
Love	
Like	
Want	
Buy	
Sell	
Read	
Write	
Drink	
Eat	
Open	
Close	
Look at	
Look for	
Find	
Start	
Stop	
Pull	

17. Essential Verbs
/ Esas fiiller

itmek

Push	
Send	
Receive	
Turn on	
Turn off	
Listen to	
Speak	
Do	
Drive	
Feel	
Know	
Leave	
Live	
Make	
Meet	
Need	
Pay	
Play	
Remember	
Repeat	
Say	
Sit	
Sleep	

17. Essential Verbs / Esas fiiller

Study	Öğrenmek
Take	
Think	
Understand	
Wait	
Watch	
There is	
There are	
I am tall	
You are short	
He is thin	
We are big	
They are intelligent	
I am at home	
You are at school	
We are at the store	
I get a prize	
I go to the movies	
I have a nice car	
I listen to the music	
I watch TV.	
I like this book	
There are ten children in the park	

18. Interrogative Words
/ Soru zamirleri

How many ...?   Kaç ...?

How much ...?

How ...?

What ...?

When ...?

Where ...?

Which ...?

Who ...?

Whose ...?

Whom ...? / To whom ...?

Why ...?

Because ...

19. Linking Words
/ Bağlaçlar

And   ve / ile

But

Or

Either ... or

Neither ... nor

Yes

No

So

While

20. The Prepositions / Edatlar

About	hakkında
Above	
Across	
At	
Behind	
Below	
Between	
By	
Down	
During	
For	
From	
In	
In front of	
Into	

20. The Prepositions
/ Edatlar

Near	*yakında*
Next to	
Of	
On	
Out	
Over	
Per	
Through	
To	
Under	
Up	
With	
Without	
The cat is in the box	
The vase is on the table	
Somebody is at the door	

21. Giving Directions / Yön göstermek / Talimat vermek

English	Turkish
At the corner	Köşede
Far	
Near	
Go straight ahead	
Left	
Right	
Turn left	
Turn right	
Go straight one block	
After the traffic light, turn right	
How can I get to ...?	
Where is the ...?	
Where is the church?	
The museum is next to the shopping center	
The drugstore is in front of the building	
The supermarket is near the park	

22. The Ordinal Numbers
/ Sıra sayıları

First	Birinci
Second	
Third	
Fourth	
Fifth	
Sixth	
Seventh	
Eighth	
Ninth	
Tenth	
Eleventh	
Twelfth	
Twentieth	
Thirtieth	
The first building	
The second floor	

23. Countries, Nationalities, and Languages /
Devletler, uyrukluk ve diller

Brazil (Country)	Brezilya
Brazilian (Nationality)	
Portuguese (Language)	
Colombia	
Colombian	
Spanish	
China	
Chinese	
Chinese	
England	
English	
English	
France	
French	
French	
Germany	
German	
German	
Italy	

23. Countries, Nationalities, and Languages /
Devletler, uyrukluk ve diller

Italian

Italian

Japan

Japanese

Japanese

Mexico

Mexican

Spanish

Spain

Spanish

Spanish

United States of America (U.S.A.)

American

English

Where are you from?

I am from Brazil

I am Brazilian

I speak Portuguese

I am not from Italy

24. Indefinite Pronouns
/ Belirsiz zamirler

Anybody	Kimse, hiç kimse
Anything	
Nobody	
Nothing	
Somebody	
Something	
Everybody	
Everything	
Is anybody home?	
I don't want anything	
Nothing happened	
Somebody is in the living room	
Everything is ready	

25. The Emotions
/ Duygu

Öfkeli, kızgın

Angry

Bored

Confident

Confused

Embarrassed

Excited

Happy

Nervous

Proud

Sad

Scared

Shy

Surprised

Worried

I am happy

He is sad

They are surprised

Are you excited?

I am not bored

She is not nervous

Everybody is confident

26. Adverbs
/ Zarflar

A few	birkaç
A little	
A lot	
After	
Again	
Ago	
Also	
Always	
Before	
Enough	
Everyday	
Exactly	
Finally	
First	
Here	
Late	
Later	
Never	
Next	
Now	

26. Adverbs
/ Zarflar

Often	çoğu zaman
Once	
Only	
Outside	
Really	
Right here	
Right now	
Since	
Slowly	
Sometimes	
Soon	
Still	
Then	
There	
Today	
Tomorrow	
Tonight	
Too	
Usually	

27. Auxiliary Verbs
/ Yardımcı fiiller

Can	*bilmek*
Could	
Did	
Do	
Does	
Have to	
May	
Must	
Should	
Will	
Would	
Can you go to the movies?	
Could I have change?	
Did you work at the drugstore?	
I did not (didn't) work at the drugstore	
Do you work at the drugstore?	
I do not (don't) work at the drugstore	
Does he read the newspaper?	
He does not (doesn't) read the newspaper	
I have to do my homework	
May I help you?	
You must turn left now	
You should go to the doctor	
I will work tomorrow	
I would like a glass of wine	

28. Expressions
/ Deyimler

Peki

All right

Come in

Come here, please

Don't worry!

For example

Good luck!

Great idea!

Have a nice day!

Help yourself!

Here you are

Hurry up!

I agree

I disagree

I don't care

I don't know

I'm coming!

I'm afraid...

It's a deal!

Keep well!

Let me think

Let's go!

Right now

Sounds good!

Sure

Take a seat

Take care!

29. The Family
/ Aile

Father	Baba
Mother	
Son	
Daughter	
Brother	
Sister	
Grandfather	
Grandmother	
Uncle	
Aunt	
Cousin	
Nephew	
Niece	
Husband	
Wife	
Boyfriend	
Girlfriend	
In-laws	
Father in-law	
Mother in-law	
Brother in-law	
Sister in-law	
Step father	
Step mother	
Step brother	
Step sister	
Who is he?	
He is my brother	

30. The House
/ Ev

Oturma odası

Living room

Door

Window

Sofa

Lamp

Dining room

Table

Chair

Kitchen

Stove

Oven

Fridge

Microwave

Bedroom

Bed

Nightstand

Vanity

Chest of drawers

Closet

Bathroom

Mirror

Sink

Toilet

Bathtub

Laundry room

Driveway

Where is the living room?

The door is big

The stove is small

The kitchen is beautiful

31. The City
/ Şehir

Block	*Semt*
Building	
Church	
Movie theater	
Museum	
Park	
Drugstore	
Restaurant	
Shopping center	
Store	
Street	
Supermarket	

32. At the Supermarket
/ Mağazada

Gıda

The food

The fruits

Apple

Banana

Cherry

Grapes

Orange

Strawberry

The vegetables

Beans

Carrot

Cauliflower

Lettuce

Onion

Pepper

Potato

Tomato

The meats

Beef

Chicken

Turkey

Ham

Pork

The dairy products

Butter

Cheese

Milk

32. At the Supermarket
/ Mağazada

Yogurt	Yoğurt
Jam	
Bread	
Eggs	
Fish	
Seafood	
Can	
Cart	
Bag	
Basket	
Bottle	
Cash register	
Cashier	
Customer service	
Groceries	
How many...?	
How many oranges do you buy?	
How much does it cost?	
How much do the bananas cost?	
I want...	
I want to buy a bottle of milk	
I would like...	
I would like a bag of tomatoes	
Where is the lettuce?	
It's on aisle one	
Where are the cans of vegetables?	
They are on aisle five	

33. At the Restaurant
/ Lokantada

Waiter / waitress	Garson
Breakfast	
Lunch	
Dinner	
To eat	
To drink	
To eat breakfast	
The menu	
Appetizer	
Salad	
Soup	
Main course	
Pasta	
Rice	
French fries	
Mashed potatoes	
Baked potatoes	
Barbecue	
Fried chicken	
Steak	

33. At the Restaurant
/ Lokantada

Dessert	Tatlı
Beverages	
Coffee	
Tea	
Soda	
Lemonade	
Orange juice	
Alcoholic drinks	
Beer	
Wine	
Check	
Tip	
How may I help you?	
What would you like to order?	
May I have the menu, please?	
Could I get more water, please?	
My order is wrong	
The service here is wonderful!	
The food is delicious!	
The check, please	
The tip is included	

34. The Office
/ Ofiste

Book   Kitap

Calculator

Computer

Desk

Fax machine

File

File cabinet

Folder

Keyboard

Monitor

Mouse

Notebook

Pad

Paper

Pen

Printer

Ruler

Scissors

Screen

Stapler

Telephone

My computer is broken

There is no paper in the printer

We need to buy more folders

We don't have a copy machine

35. Jobs and Positions
/ Meslek ve görevler

Accountant	*Muhasebeci*
Architect	
Artist	
Chef	
Clerk	
Cook	
Doctor	
Engineer	
Gardener	
Graphic designer	
Lawyer	
Nurse	
Physician	
Salesperson	
Secretary	
Security guard	
Taxi driver	
Teacher	
Technician	
Tourist guide	
Travel agent	

36. Job Interview
/ İş başvurusu

İş arama

Apply for a job

Duty

Experience

Last name

First name

Full time job

Part time job

Résumé

Skill

Work

37. The Transportation
/ Taşıt araçları

Uçak

Airplane

Bicycle

Bus

Car

Helicopter

Metro

Motorcycle

Train

Truck

38. The Traffic
/ Ulaştırma

Bus stop	Otobüs durağı
Crosswalk	
Freeway, highway	
Gas station	
Intersection	
Lane	
No outlet	
One way	
Pedestrian	
Speed	
Stop sign	
To get in	
To get off	
Toll	
Traffic light	
Train station	
Two way	
U-turn	
Yield	
I get in the car	
I get off the car	
We wait for the train	

39. The Car
/ Otomobil/araba

Accelerator	*Gaz pedali*
Battery	
Hood	
Brake	
Clutch	
Engine	
Fender	
Gear box	
Headlight	
Rear view mirror	
Make	
Model	
Radiator	
Steering wheel	
Seat	
Tire	
Trunk	
Wheel	
Windshield	
Windshield wipers	
The car is broken	
I have a flat tire	
I need a new battery	
What year is the car?	
What make is the car?	
What model is the car?	
How many miles does the car have?	

40. Phone Conversations
/ Ttelefon görüşmesi

Call	Telefon etmek
Dial	
Directory	
Directory Assistance	
Extension	
Hold on, please	
I'd like to speak to...	
I'll put you through	
I'll transfer your call	
I'm calling about ...	
Just a minute	
Leave a message	
Let me see...	
Phone	
Phone number	
Ring	
Speak	
Speaking	
Take a message	
Talk	
This is...	
Who's calling?	

41. At the Post Office
/ **Postada**

Air mail   *Uçak postası*

Counter

Envelope

Letter

Mail

Parcel

Postcard

Postman, mailman

Stamp

To send

To deliver

Delivery

To pick up

Address

I want to send a letter

I would like to pick up a parcel

How much do the stamps cost?

Do you sell postcards?

42. At the Bank
/ Bankada

Account	Hesap
ATM	
Bank statement	
Bank teller	
Cash	
Checkbook	
Checking account	
Credit card	
Debit card	
Deposit slip	
Savings account	
To deposit	
To save	
To transfer	
To withdraw	
Transactions	
Withdrawal slip	
I want to make a deposit	
Do you have a savings account?	
I have a checking account	
What is your credit card number?	
I don't have an ATM card	
Where are the deposit slips?	

43. At the Airport
/ Hava limanında

Varış

Arrival

Concourse

Customs

Departure

Destination

Entrance

Exit

First class

Flight

Gate

Immigrations office

Luggage

Passport

Restrooms

Suitcase

To arrive

To depart

To travel

Trip

Where are you traveling?

May I have your ticket, please?

I need you passport, please

My flight number is ...

Where is gate number ...?

The flight is delayed

The flight is on time

44. At the Hotel
/ Otelde

Double room	İki kişilik oda
Single room	
Bell desk	
Bellman	
Elevator	
Reception	
Receptionist	
Reservation	
Stairway	
Swimming pool	
Tours desk	
Valet parking	
To check-in	
To check-out	
I would like to make a reservation	
I want a single room	
I would like to check-in	

45. The Clothes
/ Giyim

Mayo

Bathing suit

Belt

Blouse

Coat

Dress

Gloves

Hat

Jacket

Pants

Purse

Scarf

Shirt

Shoes

Shorts

Skirt

Socks

Suit

Suitcase

The size

Small

Medium

Large

Big sizes

46. At the Shopping Center / Alış-veriş merkezinde

English	Turkish
Department store	Büyük mağaza
Ladies	
Men	
Juniors	
Kids	
Ladies' department	
Jewelry	
Fitting room	
Elevator	
Escalator	
How may I help you?	
I'm looking for ...	
I'm just looking	
Where is the fitting room?	
It fits well	
It doesn't fit well	
May I pay here?	
I want to exchange this	
I want to return this	
I like ...	
I like this blouse	
I don't like ...	
I don't like these pants	

47. At the Drugstore
/ Eczanede

Antiseptic	Antiseptik / desinfektan (ilacı)
Adhesive bandage	
Antibiotic	
Aspirin	
Bandage	
Cold medicine	
Cough syrup	
Medication	
Ointment	
OTC (Over The Counter) medication	
Painkiller	
Pills	
Prescription	
Tablets	
Thermometer	
Cotton	

48. The Parts of the Body
/ Beden

Ankle	*Ayak bileği*
Arm	
Back	
Buttock	
Calf	
Chest	
Elbow	
Feet	
Finger	
Foot	
Forearm	
Hand	
Head	
Hip	
Knee	
Leg	
Neck	
Shoulder	
Stomach	
Thigh	
Toe	
Waist	
Wrist	

49. Health Problems
/ Sağlık problemleri

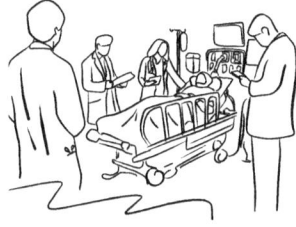

Sırtım ağrıyor

Backache	
Cold	
Fever	
Hurt	
Indigestion	
Injury	
Pain	
Pulse	
Sick	
Sneeze	
Sore throat	
Toothache	
I have a headache	
I have a stomachache	
I have pain in my knee	
I hurt my hand	
I've got a cold	
My foot hurts	

50. The Animals
/ Hayvanlar

Bear	Ayı
Bird	
Cat	
Chicken	
Cow	
Dog	
Duck	
Elephant	
Fish	
Horse	
Lizard	
Lion	
Monkey	
Mouse	
Rat	
Tiger	

EXERCISE!

Write the English translation.

Keep practicing at:
QuickLanguages.com

1. Greetings
/ Selam

Turkish	English
Merhaba / Selam!	Hi! / Hello!
Günaydın!	
İyi günler!	
İyi akşamlar! / İyi geceler!	
Nasılsın?	
İyi	
Pek iyi	
Teşekkür ederim / Teşekkürler	
Çok teşekkür	
Rica ederim	
İyi, sağ ol	
Ya sen?	
Görüşmek üzere!	
Görüşürüz!	
Yarın görüşürüz!	
Allahaısmarladık	
Güle güle!	

2. Introductions and Courtesy Expressions / **Tanışma ve nezaket deyimleri**

Adınız ne?	*What is your name?*
Adım ...	
Siz kimsiniz?	
Ben ...	
Bu efendi kimdir?/Bu bayan kimdir?	
Bu efendi ... / Bu bayan ...	
Tanıştığımızdan memnun oldum	
Ben de memnun oldum	
Memnuniyet benim	
Özür dilerim/Affedersiniz	
Lütfen / Efendim	
Bir an, lütfen	
Hoş geldin!	
Buyurunuz	
Tekrar söyler misiniz, lütfen?	
Anlayamam	
Biraz anlıyorum	
Daha yavaş konuşabilir misiniz, lütfen?	
İspanyolca biliyor musunuz?	
Merhaba kelimesinin İspanyolca'sı nasıl?	
Bu ne demek?	
Biraz İspanyolca biliyorum	

3. Ways to Address to a Person
/ Bir kimseye hitap kelimeleri

Bayan / Bayan efendi	Madam / Ma'am
Bayan	
Bayan	
Efendi / Beyefendi / Bay / Bey	
Bayan / Bayan efendi	
Efendi/Beyefendi	
Doktor	

4. The Articles
/ Yoktur

Ø	The
araba	
arabalar	
ev	
evler	
bir	
bir araba	
bir ev	
bir	
bir fil	
bir elma	
birkaç	
birkaç araba / birkaç arabalar	
birkaç ev/ birkaç evler	

5. The Subject Pronouns
/ Şahıs zamirleri

Ben	I
Sen	
O	
O	
O	
Biz	
Siz	
Onlar	

6. The Possessive Adjectives
/ İyelik zamirleri

Benim	My
Senin	
Onun	
Onun	
Onun	
Bizim	
Sizin	
Onların	
(Benim) arabam	
(Senin) kitabın	
(Onun) televizyonu	
(Bizim) evimiz	

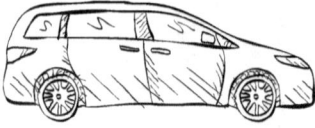

7. The Demonstrative Adjectives / İşaret zamirleri

Bu	This
Bu kitap	
Bu gömlek	
Bunlar	
Bu kitaplar	
Bu gömlekler	
Şu	
Şu masa	
Şu araba	
Şunlar	
Şu masalar	
Şu arabalar	

8. The Possessive Pronouns / İyelik zamirleri

Benim	Mine
Senin	
Onun	
Onun	
Onun	
Bizim	
Sizin	
Onların	
Araba benim	
Kitap senin	
Bu televizyon onundur	
Bu ev bizim	

9. The Cardinal Numbers
/ Sayı sıfatları

Sıfır	*0 / Zero*
Bir	
İki	
Üç	
Dört	
Beş	
Altı	
Yedi	
Sekiz	
Dokuz	
On	
On bir	
On iki	
On üç	
On dört	
On beş	
On altı	
On yedi	
On sekiz	
On dokuz	
Yirmi	
Yirmi bir	
Otuz	
Kırk	
Elli	
Altmış	

1. 2. 3. 4.
5. 6. 7. 8.
9. 0.

9. The Cardinal Numbers
/ Sayı sıfatları

Yetmiş	70 / Seventy
Seksen	
Doksan	
Yüz	
Yüz bir	
İki yüz	
Üç yüz	
Dört yüz	
Beş yüz	
Altı yüz	
Yedi yüz	
Sekiz yüz	
Dokuz yüz	
Bin	
On bin	
Yüz bin	
Bir milyon	
Bir milyar	
Kırk beş	
Yüz yirmi sekiz	
Bin dokuz yüz altmış üç	
Altı bin otuz yedi	
On bir bin	
İki yüz yetmiş dokuz bin	
İki milyon	

10. The Time
/ Saat

Saat (duvar saati)

The clock

Saat (el saati)

Saat kaç?

Saat ...

Saat bir (1:00)

Saat iki (2:00)

Saat üç çeyrek / Saat üçü on beş geçiyor (3:15)

Saat dört buçuk (4:30)

Saat beş kırk beş / Saat altıya on beş var (5:45)

Saat altı elli / Saat yediye on kalıyor (6:50)

Öğle vakti (12:00)

Gece yarısı (00:00)

Sabah

Öğleden sonra

Akşam

Gece

Saat kaçta ...?

Konser saat kaçta başlıyor ?

Saat ...

Saat 7:10 (saat yediyi on geçe)

SUNDAY
MONDAY
TUESDAY
WEDNESDAY
THURSDAY
FRIDAY
SATURDAY

11. The Days of the Week / Hafta günleri

Pazartesi	Monday
Salı	
Çarşamba	
Perşembe	
Cuma	
Cumartesi	
Pazar	
Bugün günlerden hangi gün?	

12. The Months of the Year / Yılın ayları

HELLO February June October
HELLO March July November
HELLO April August December
HELLO May September

Ocak	January
Şubat	
Mart	
Nisan	
Mayıs	
Haziran	
Temmuz	
Ağustos	
Eylül	
Ekim	
Kasım	
Aralık	
Bugün ayın kaçı?	

13. The Weather
/ Hava

Güneşli	Sunny
Bulutlu	
Yağmurlu	
Nemli	
Kuru	
Soğuk	
Sıcak	
Çok sıcak	
Yağmur	
Kar	
Bugün hava nasıl?	
Hava güzel	
Güneşli	
Kışın hava soğuk	
Yağmur yağıyor	
Kar yağıyor	
Üşüyorum	

14. The Seasons / Mevsimler

İlk bahar	*Spring*
Yaz	
Son bahar	
Kış	

15. The Colors / Renkler

Sarı	*Yellow*
Kırmızı	
Mavi	
Yeşil	
Turuncu	
Kahverengi	
Pembe	
Mor	
Siyah	
Beyaz	
Gri	
Açık	
Koyu	
Açık yeşil	
Portakal renkli kitap	
Kahverengi ayakkabı	
Bluzum beyaz	
....rengi ne? / Hangi renk?	
En çok sevdiğin renk hangisi? / En sevdiğin renk ne?	

16. The Parts of the Face
/ Yüz

Cheek

Yanak

Çene

Kulak

Göz

Alın

Saç

Dudak

Ağız

Burun

Cilt

Dişler

Diş

Sarı/ sarşın / sarı saçlı

Kumral

Kır saçlı

Kızıl saçlı / kırmızı saçlı

Uzun saçlı

Kısa saçlı

Düz saçlı

Kıvırcık saçlı

John sarı / John sarı saçlı

Karen uzun saçlı

O yeşil gözlü

O mavi gözlü bayan

Gözleri iri ve kahverengi

17. Essential Verbs
/ Esas fiiller

Olmak	Be
Gitmek	
Gelmek	
Sahip olmak	
Almak	
Yardım etmek	
Sevmek	
Beğenmek	
İstemek	
Satın almak	
Satmak	
Okumak	
Yazmak	
İçmek	
Yemek	
Açmak	
Kapatmak	
Bakmak	
Aramak	
Bulmak	
Başlamak	
Birakmak	
Çekmek	

17. Essential Verbs
/ Esas fiiller

İtmek

Göndermek

Almak

Açmak

Söndürmek

Dinlemek

Konuşmak

Yapmak

Araba kullanmak (sürmek)

Hissetmek

Bilmek

Terk etmek, çıkmak

Yaşamak

Hazırlamak

Tanışmak

İhtiyacı olmak/Muhtaç olmak

Ödemek

Oynamak

Hatırlamak

Tekrarlamak

Söylemek

Oturmak

Uyumak

17. Essential Verbs
/ Esas fiiller

Öğrenmek	Study
Almak	
Düşünmek	
Anlamak	
Beklemek	
İzlemek	
Var/Bulunuyor	
Var/Bulunuyor	
Ben uzun boyluyum	
Sen kısa boylusun	
O zayıf.	
Biz büyüküz	
Onlar akıllıdırlar	
Ben evdeyim	
Sen okuldasın	
Biz mağazadayız	
(Ben bir) ödül kazanıyorum	
Sinemaya gidiyorum	
Benim güzel bir arabam var	
Müzik dinliyorum	
Televizyon izliyorum	
Bu kitabı beğeniyorum	
Parkta on çocuk var	

18. Interrogative Words
/ Soru zamirleri

Kaç ....?	How many ...?
Ne kadar ....?	
Nasıl...?	
Ne...?	
Ne zaman...?	
Nerede/Nereye/Nereden...?	
Hangi...?	
Kim...?	
Kimin...?	
Kimi...? / Kime ...?	
Neden/Niçin...?	
Çünkü....	

19. Linking Words
/ Bağlaçlar

ve / ile	And
ama / fakat	
veya / yoksa	
gerek ... gerek	
ne ... ne	
Evet	
Hayır	
o halde / demek ki / yani	
zaman/süre /... esnasında	

20. The Prepositions
/ Edatlar

hakkında	About
üzerinde	
karşı/karşısında	
-da, '-de, '-a, '-e, '-ya, '-ye	
arakada / arkasında / -in arkasinda	
altında	
arasında	
ile	
aşağıda	
....zamanında / ... esnasında / ... sırasında	
için	
-den	
içinde	
önünde	
içinde	

20. The Prepositions
/ Edatlar

yakında	Near
yanında	
_l, _in, _un, ün....	
üstünde/üzerinde	
dışarıda	
üstünde/üzerinde	
başına/her biri için	
-den	
doğru	
altında	
yukarıya	
ile	
-siz, '-sız, '-suz, '-süz	
Kedi kutunun içindedir	
Vazo masanın üstündedir	
Biri kapının önündedir	

21. Giving Directions
/ Yön göstermek /
Talimat vermek

Köşede	*At the corner*
-den uzak	
-ye yakın	
Doğru/düz gidiniz	
Sola	
Sağa	
Sola çeviriniz	
Sağa çeviriniz	
Bundan sonraki sokağa kadar doğruya devam ediniz	
Trafik ışığından sonra sağa çeviriniz	
-ye nasıl ulaşabilirim/ gidebilirim?	
... Nerede bulunuyor?	
Kilise nerede bulunuyor ? / Kilise nerede?	
Müze alış-veriş merkezinin yanında bulunuyor	
Eczane binanın karşısında bulunuyor	
Süpermarket parkın yakınındadır	

22. The Ordinal Numbers
/ Sıra sayıları

Birinci	First
İkinci	
Üçüncü	
Dördüncü	
Beşinci	
Altıncı	
Yedinci	
Sekizinci	
Dokuzuncu	
Onuncu	
On birinci	
On ikinci	
Yirminci	
Otuzuncu	
Birinci bina	
İkinci kat	

23. Countries, Nationalities, and Languages /
Devletler, uyrukluk ve diller

Brezilya	Brazil (Country)
Brezilyalı	
Portekizce	
Kolombiya	
Kolombiya'lı	
İspanyolca	
Çin	
Çin	
Çince	
İngiltere	
İngiliz	
İngilizce	
Fransa	
Fransız	
Fransızca	
Almanya	
Alman	
Almanca	
İtalya	

23. Countries, Nationalities, and Languages /
Devletler, uyrukluk ve diller

İtalyan/İtalyalı	Italian
İtalyanca	
Japonya	
Japon/Japonyalı	
Japonca	
Meksika	
Meksikalı	
İspanyolca	
İspanya	
İspanyol	
İspanyolca	
Amerika Birleşik Devletleri (ABD)	
Amerikan/Amerikalı	
İngilizce	
Nerelisiniz?	
Brezilya'dan geliyorum	
Ben brezilyalıyım / Ben brezilyanım	
Portekizce biliyorum	
Ben italyan değilim	

24. Indefinite Pronouns
/ Belirsiz zamirler

kimse, hiç kimse	Anybody
bir şey	
hiç kimse	
hiçbir şey	
biri (si)	
bir şey	
herkes	
her şey	
Evde biri (si) var mı?	
Bir şey istemem / Bir şey istemiyorum	
Hiç bir şey olmadı	
Salonda biri (si) var	
Her şey hazır	

25. The Emotions
/ Duygu

Öfkeli, kızgın

Bıkkın

Kendinden emin

Şaşkın / karışık / şaşırmış

Utangaç

Heyecanlı

Neşeli

Sinirli

Gururlu

Üzgün

Korkak

Utangaç / Çekingen

Şaşkın / Hayret içinde

Endişeli

Ben memnunum / mutluyum

O üzüntülü

(Onlar) Şaşkındırlar

Sen heyecanlandın mı?

Bıkkın değilim

(o) Sinirli değil

Kerkes kendine emin

26. Adverbs / Zarflar

birkaç	A few
az	
çok	
sonra	
tekrar	
önce	
yine	
daima / her zaman	
önce	
yeter	
her gün	
tam / doğru	
eninde sonunda	
ilk önce	
burada	
geç	
daha sonra	
hiçbir zaman	
bundan sonraki	
şimdi	

26. Adverbs
/ Zarflar

çoğu zaman   *Often*

bir kez

yalnız / sadece

dışarıda

Sahi / gerçekten / sahiden

tam bu yerde

hemen

o zamandan beri

yavaş

ara sıra / bazen

yakinda

henüz

o zaman / ondan sonra

orada

bugün

yarın

bu akşam

da / de

genellikle

27. Auxiliary Verbs
/ Yardımcı fiiller

bilmek	*Can*
olabilir	
olmak, sahip olmak	
∅	
olmak	
-meye mecbur olmak, mecbur	
-ebilmek	
-meli	
-meli	
olmak, -ecek	
Olur	
Sinemaya gelebilir (gidebilirmisin) misin?	
Para bozdurabilir misiniz?	
Eczanede mi çalışmışstın?	
Eczanede çalışmadım	
Eczanede mi çalışıyorsun?	
Eczanede çalışmıyorum	
(O) Gazeteyi okuyor mu?	
(O) Gazeteyi okumuyor	
Ev ödevimi yazmam gerek (lazım / yazmalıyım)	
Sana yardım edebilir miyim?	
Şimdi sola çevirmen gerek (lazım / çevirmelisin)?	
Doktora gitmen gerek (lazım / gitmelisin)	
Yarın çalışacağım	
Bir bardak şarap isterim	

28. Expressions
/ Deyimler

All right

Peki

Buyurun / Buyurunuz

Buraya geliniz lütfen

Sıkılma

Örneğin / mesela

Bol şans dilerim!

Harika!

İyi günler!

Buyurun!

Buyurun!

Acele et!

Kabul ediyorum

Kabul etmiyorum

Bu beni ilgilendirmez

Bilmem

Geliyorum

-den korkuyorum

Tamam! / Oldu!

Kendine bak!

Biraz düşüneyim

Gidelim!

Hemen / şimdi / derhal

Pek iyi!

Muhakkak

Buyurun, oturunuz

Kendine iyi bak!

29. The Family
/ Aile

Baba	Father
Anne	
Oğul	
Kız	
Kardeş	
Kız kardeşi	
Dede	
Büyük anne / anneanne	
Amca	
Hala	
Kuzin / kuzen	
Yeğen	
Kardeş kızı (kiz) yeğen	
Eş, koca	
Eş, karı	
Nişanlı / arkadaş	
Nişanlı, kız arkadaşı	
Dünür	
Kaynata (kayınpeder)	
Kaynana (kayınvalide)	
Kayınbirader / enişte / bacanak	
Görümce / baldız / elti / yenge	
Üvey baba / babalık	
Üvey ana / analık	
Üvey kardeş	
Üvey kız kardeş	
O kimdir?	
O kardeşimdir	

30. The House
/ Ev

Living room

Oturma odası
Kapı
Pencere
Kanepe
Lamba
Yemek odası
Masa
İskemle, sandalye
Mutfak
Soba
Fırın
Buzdolabı
Mikrodalga sobası
Yatak odası
Yatak
Komodin
Tuvalet masası
Komot
Dolap
Banyo
Ayna
Lavabo
Tuvalet
Küvet
Çamaşırhane
Park yeri
Oturma odası nerede?
Kapı büyük
Soba küçük
Mutfak güzel

31. The City
/ Şehir

Semt	Block
Bina	
Kilise	
Sinema	
Müze	
Park	
Eczane	
Lokanta	
Alış-veriş merkezi	
Mağaza	
Sokak, cadde	
Süpermarket	

32. At the Supermarket
/ Mağazada

Gıda

The food

Meyve

Elma

Muz

Kiraz

Üzüm

Portakal

Çilek

Sebze

Fasulye

Havuç

Karnabahar

Salata / marul

Soğan

Biber

Patates

Domates

Et

Dana eti

Piliç / tavuk eti

Hindi

Jambon

Domuz eti

Süt ürünleri

Tereyağı

Peynir

Süt

32. At the Supermarket / Mağazada

Yoğurt	Yogurt
Reçel	
Ekmek	
Yumurta	
Balık	
Deniz hayvanları	
Konserve	
Pazar arabası	
Torba	
Sepet	
Şişe	
Kasa	
Veznedar	
Müşteri hizmetleri	
Bakkaliye	
Kaç/ne kadar ....?	
Kaç portakal alıyorsunuz?	
Fiyatı ne kadar?	
Muzlarin fıyatı kaç?	
... istiyorum	
Bir şişe süt almak istiyorum	
... isterim	
1 poşet domates almak istiyorum	
Yeşil salata nerede?	
Birinci sırada	
Sebze konserveleri nerede?	
Beşinci sırada	

33. At the Restaurant
/ Lokantada

Garson	Waiter / waitress
Kahvaltı	
Öğle yemeği	
Akşam yemeği	
Yemek	
İçmek	
Kahvaltı yapmak	
Yemek listesi / menü	
Meze	
Salata	
Çorba	
Yemek	
Makarna	
Pirinç	
Kızartılmış patates	
Patates ezmesi	
Patates kızartması	
Izgara	
Piliç kızartması	
Pirzola	

33. At the Restaurant
/ Lokantada

Tatlı	Dessert
İçecekler	
Kahve	
Çay	
Gazoz	
Limonata	
Portakal suyu	
Alkollü içkiler	
Bira	
Şarap	
Hesap	
Bahşiş	
Size yardım edebilir miyim?	
Siparişinizi alabilir miyim?	
Yemek listesini verir misiniz, lütfen?	
Biraz su getiri misiniz, lütfen?	
Bunu ısmarlamış değilim	
Burada hizmet çok iyi	
Yemek çok lezzetli	
Hesap lütfen	
Bahşiş dahil	

34. The Office
/ Ofiste

Kitap   *Book*

Hesap makinesi

Bilgisayar

Büro

Faks makinesi

Dosya

Dosya dolabı

Dosya

Klavye

Monitör

Fare

Karne

Fare altlığı

Kağıt

Tükenmez

Yazıcı

Cetvel

Makas

Ekran

Tel zımba

Telefon

Bilgisayarım arızalı

Yazıcıda kağıt yok

Daha çok dosya almamız gerek

Kopya makinemiz yok

35. Jobs and Positions / Meslek ve görevler

Muhasebeci	*Accountant*
Mimar	
Artist	
Baş aşçı	
Memur / görevli	
Aşçı	
Doktor	
Mühendis	
Bahçıvan	
Dizayner / tasarımcı	
Avukat	
Hemşire	
Hekim	
Satıcı	
Sekreter	
Koruma memuru	
Taksi sürücüsü	
Öğretmen	
Teknisyen	
Rehber	
Turizm acentesi	

36. Job Interview
/ İş başvurusu

İş arama	Apply for a job
Pozisyon	
Tecrübe	
Soyadı	
Ad	
Tam mesai saatler	
Saatlik iş	
Özgeçmiş	
Yetenekler	
Çalışmak / iş	

37. The Transportation
/ Taşıt araçları

Uçak	Airplane
Bisiklet	
Otobüs	
Oto/araba	
Helikopter	
Metro	
Motosiklet	
Tren	
Kamyon	

38. The Traffic / Ulaştırma

Otobüs durağı	Bus stop
Yaya geçidi	
Otoyol	
Benzin istasyonu	
Kavşak	
Yol şeridi	
Çıkmaz yol	
Tek istikametli yol	
Yaya	
Sürat / Hız	
Stop	
Binmek	
İnmek	
Yol ücreti	
Trafik ışıkları	
Istasyon	
İki istikametli yol	
Dönüş	
Yer vermek	
Arabaya binmek	
Arabadan inmek	
Treni bekliyoruz	

39. The Car
/ Otomobil/araba

Gaz pedalı	Accelerator
Akü	
Motor kapağı	
Fren	
Debriyaj	
Motor	
Tampon	
Vites kutusu	
Far	
Ayna	
Marka	
Model	
Radyatör	
Direksiyon simidi	
Koltuk	
Lastik	
Bagaj	
Tekerlek	
Ön cam	
Ön cam siperi	
Araba arızalandı	
Lastik patladı	
Yeni aküye ihtiyacım var	
Otonun imalat yılı hangisi?	
Otonun markası ne?	
Otonun modeli ne?	
Otomobilin kaç kilometresi var?	

40. Phone Conversations / Ttelefon görüşmesi

Telefon etmek	Call
Çevirmek	
Telefon rehberi	
Enformasyon	
Uzatma numarası	
Bir saniye, lütfen	
.... İle görüşebilir miyim	
Bağlıyorum	
Görüşmenizi İletiyorum	
.... İle ilgili olarak telefon ediyorum	
Biraz bekler misiniz, lütfen	
Mesajınız olacak mı?	
Bakayım	
Telefonla aramak	
Telefon numarası	
Telefon etmek	
Seslenmek	
Telefonda	
Mesaj iletmek	
Konuşmak	
Telefonda	
Kiminle görüşüyorum?	

41. At the Post Office
/ Postada

Uçak postası — Air mail

Gişe

Zarf

Mektup

Yazışma

Koli

Kart postal

Postacı

Posta pulu / pul

Göndermek

Sevk etmek / teslim etmek / temin etmek

Sevk

Almak

Adres

Mektup göndermek istiyorum.

Bir koli (paket) almak istiyorum.

Pulların fiyatı ne kadar?

Kart postal(lar) satıyor musunuz?

42. At the Bank / Bankada

Hesap	Account
Bankamatik / paramatik	
Banka beyanı	
Veznedar / kasiyer	
Nakit para	
Çek defteri	
Cari hesap	
Kredi kartı	
Zimmet kartı	
Depozito bordrosu / ödeme belgesi	
Tasarruf hesabı	
Yatırmak	
Tasarruf etmek	
Havale etmek	
Çekmek	
Banka işlemi	
Çekme bordrosu	
Depozito hesabı açtırmak istiyorum	
Tasarruf hesabınız var mı?	
Cari hesabım var	
Kredi kartınızın numarası ne?	
Bankamatik kartım yok?	
Depozito tahsil senetleri nerede?	

43. At the Airport
/ Hava limanında

Varış

Bekleme salonu

Gümrük

Kalkış

Gidilecek yer / yolculuk hedefi

Giriş

Çıkış

Birinci mevki

Uçuş

Terminal

İltica Şubesi

Bagaj

Pasaport

Tuvalet

Valiz

Varmak

Kalkmak

Yolculuk etmek / seyahat yapmak

Yolculuk/Seyahat

Nereye yolculuk ediyorsunuz? /
Yolculuk nereye?

Biletinizi gösterir misiniz, lütfen?

Pasaportunuzu verir misiniz,
lütfen

Uçuşun numarası ...

... Numaralı terminal nerede?

Uçuşun gecikmesi var

Uçuş tam zamanında geliyor

44. At the Hotel
/ Otelde

İki kişilik oda	Double room
Tek kişilik oda	
Resepsiyon	
Otel garsonu	
Asansör	
Resepsiyon	
Resepsiyon görevlisi	
Rezervasyon	
Merdiven	
Yüzme havuzu	
Seyahat acentesi	
Park etme hizmeti	
Işlem yapmak	
Otelden ayrılmak	
Rezervasyon yapmak istiyorum	
Tek kişilik oda istiyorum	
Otele yerleşmek istiyorum	

45. The Clothes
/ Giyim

Bathing suit

Mayo

Kemer

Bluz

Palto

Elbise

Eldiven

Şapka

Ceket

Pantolon

Cüzdan / para kesesi

Şal

Gömlek

Ayakkabı

Şort

Etek

Çorap

Takım

Valiz

Boy

Küçük

Orta

Büyük

Büyük boy

46. At the Shopping Center / Alış-veriş merkezinde

Turkish	English
Büyük mağaza	Department store
Bayanlar	
Baylar	
Gençler	
Çocuklar	
bayan giyimi	
Mücevherat	
Prova	
Asansör	
Yürüyen merdiven	
Yardım edebilir miyim?	
... arıyorum	
Yalnız bakıyorum ...	
Prova odası nerede?	
Bana yakışıyor	
Bana yakışmıyor	
Burada ödeyebilir miyim?	
Bunu değiştirmek istiyorum	
Bunu geri vermek istiyorum	
Hoşuma gidiyor ...	
Bu bluz hoşuma gidiyor	
Hoşuma gitmiyor	
Bu pantolon hoşuma gitmiyor	

47. At the Drugstore
/ Eczanede

Antiseptik / desinfektan (ilacı)	Antiseptic
Yara bandı	
Antibiyotik	
Aspirin	
Sargı	
Soğuk alma ilacı	
Öksürük şurubu	
İlaçlar	
Merhem	
Reçetesiz ilaçlar	
Ağrı kesici	
Haplar	
Reçete	
Tabletler	
Termometre	
Pamuk	

48. The Parts of the Body
/ Beden

Ayak bileği	Ankle
Kol	
Sırt	
Kıç	
Baldır	
Göğüs	
Dirsek	
Ayaklar	
Parmak	
Ayak	
Kol	
El	
Baş	
Kalça	
Diz	
Ayak	
Boyun	
Omuz	
Mide	
But	
Ayak parmağı	
Bel	
Bilek	

49. Health Problems
/ Sağlık problemleri

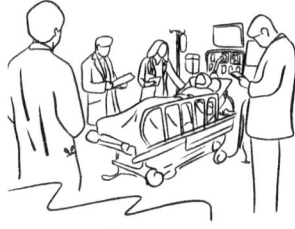

Sırtım ağrıyor	Backache
Soğuk alma	
Ateş	
Ağrımak / acımak	
Mide bozukluğu	
Yara	
Ağrı	
Nabız	
Hasta	
Nezle	
Boğaz ağrısı	
Diş ağrısı	
Baş ağrısı	
Mide ağrısı	
Dizim ağrıyor	
Elimi yaraladım	
Üşütüm	
Ayağım ağrıyor	

50. The Animals
/ Hayvanlar

Ayı	Bear
Kuş	
Kedi	
Piliç	
İnek	
Köpek	
Ördek	
Fil	
Balık	
At	
Kertenkele	
Aslan	
Maymun	
Sıçan	
Fare	
Kaplan	

QUICK LANGUAGES

MULTI-LANGUAGE PHRASEBOOK COLLECTION

SPEAK ANY LANGUAGE NOW!

QUICK LANGUAGES PHRASEBOOK COLLECTION
AVAILABLE TITLES

1. ENGLISH-SPANISH & SPANISH-ENGLISH
2. ENGLISH-ITALIAN & ITALIAN-ENGLISH
3. ENGLISH-FRENCH & FRENCH-ENGLISH
4. ENGLISH-GERMAN & GERMAN-ENGLISH
5. ENGLISH-PORTUGUESE & PORTUGUESE-ENGLISH
6. ENGLISH-CHINESE & CHINESE-ENGLISH
7. ENGLISH-ARABIC & ARABIC-ENGLISH
8. ENGLISH-JAPANESE & JAPANESE-ENGLISH
9. ENGLISH-KOREAN & KOREAN-ENGLISH
10. ENGLISH-RUSSIAN & RUSSIAN-ENGLISH
11. ENGLISH-TURKISH & TURKISH-ENGLISH

GET THE AUDIOVISUAL AND INTERACTIVE CONTENT AT QuickLanguages.com

www.ingramcontent.com/pod-product-compliance
Lightning Source LLC
LaVergne TN
LVHW021452080426
835509LV00018B/2256